Animals Close Up

HAMSTERS CLOSE UP

By Seth Lynch

Gareth Stevens Publishing

Please visit our website, www.garethstevens.com. For a free color catalog of all our high-quality books, call toll free 1-800-542-2595 or fax 1-877-542-2596.

Library of Congress Cataloging-in-Publication Data
Names: Lynch, Seth, author.
Title: Hamsters close up / Seth Lynch.
Description: New York : Gareth Stevens Publishing, [2023] | Series: Animals close up | Includes index.
Identifiers: LCCN 2021040568 (print) | LCCN 2021040569 (ebook) | ISBN 9781538281321 (set) | ISBN 9781538281338 (library binding) | ISBN 9781538281314 (paperback) | ISBN 9781538281345 (ebook)
Subjects: LCSH: Hamsters–Juvenile literature.
Classification: LCC QL737.R666 L95 2023 (print) | LCC QL737.R666 (ebook) | DDC 599.35/6–dc23
LC record available at https://lccn.loc.gov/2021040568
LC ebook record available at https://lccn.loc.gov/2021040569

First Edition

Published in 2023 by
Gareth Stevens Publishing
29 East 21st Street
New York, NY 10010

Editor: Kristen Nelson
Designer: Rachel Rising

Photo credits: Cover, p.1 Karen Grigoryan/Shutterstock.com; p. 5 Daria_Cherry/Shutterstock.com; p. 7 Sharon Snider/Shutterstock.com; p. 9 Alexruss/Shutterstock.com; p. 11 Mary Swift/Shutterstock.com; pp. 13,24 Una Silkane/Shutterstock.com; p. 15 MarisaJ/Shutterstock.com; p. 17 Olena Kurashova/Shutterstock.com; pp. 19, 24 Anna Plsk/Shutterstock.com; pp. 21, 24 Kuttelvaserova Stuchelova/Shutterstock.com; p. 23 Dr David Sing/Shutterstock.com.

Printed in the United States of America

CPSIA compliance information: Batch #CSGS23: For further information contact Gareth Stevens, New York, New York at 1-800-542-2595.

Contents

There are 24 kinds of hamster.

Some are kept as pets.
The teddy bear hamster
is a pet.

Hamsters have
small ears.
The ears are furry.

They have two eyes.
These don't see well.

Hamsters' teeth grow fast.

They chew wood.
This keeps their
teeth short.

They have short legs.
Tails are short too.

Feet are wide.
They have claws.

Fur can be black or red.
It can be white or gray.
It can be a mix!

Skin under the fur is pink.

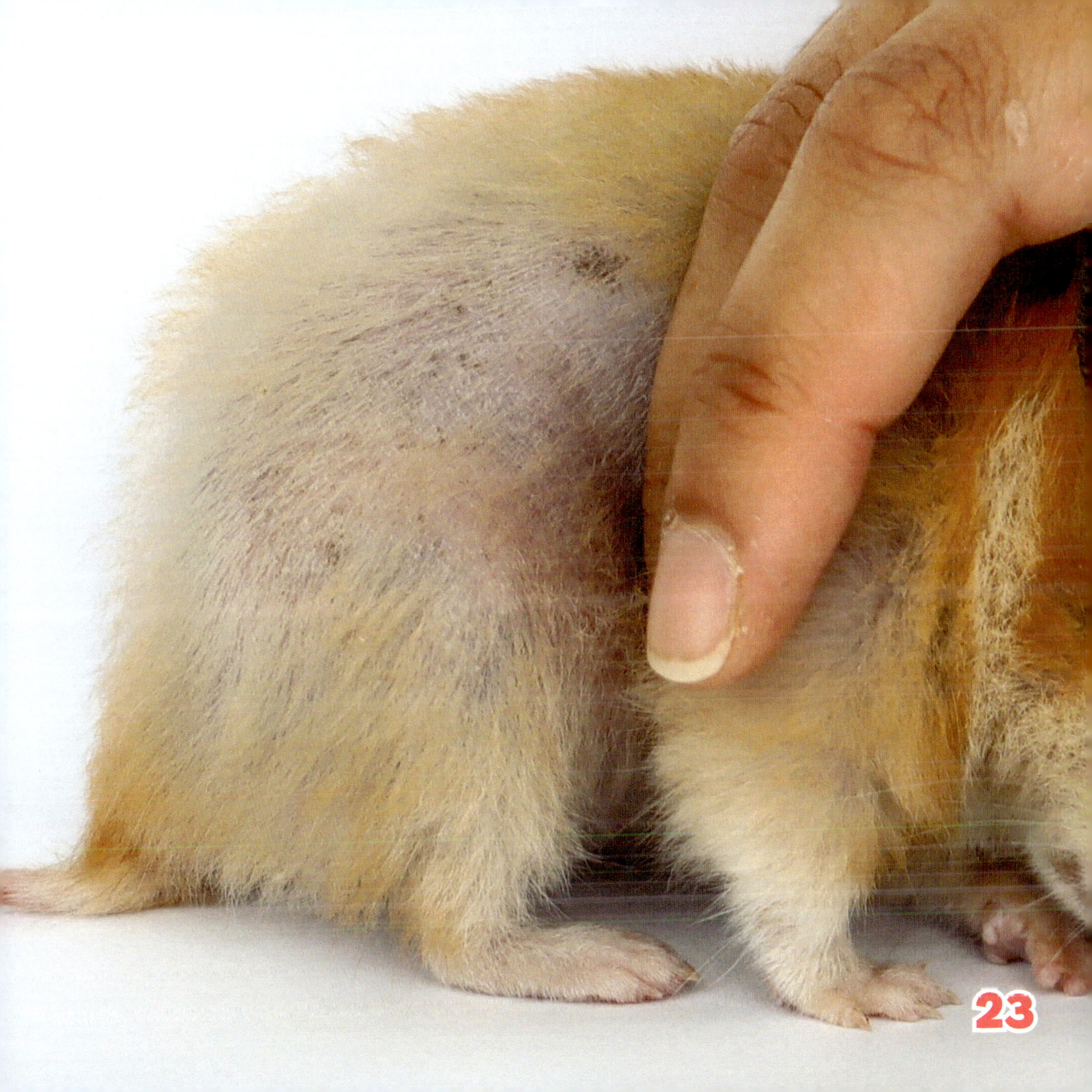

Words to Know

claws

fur

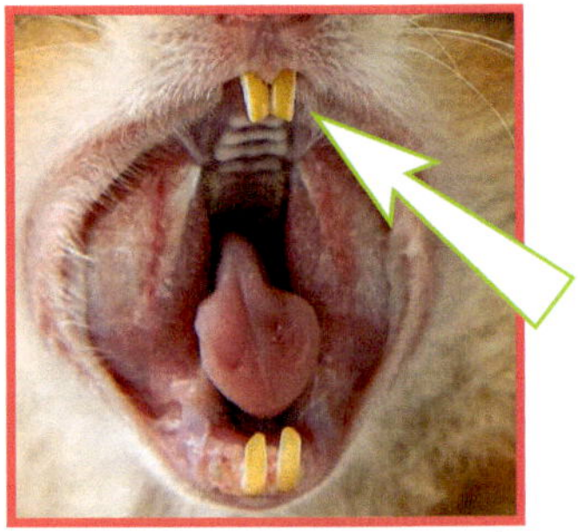

teeth

Index